Highlights

T0015912

SILLIEST HIDDEN PICTURES PUZZLES EVER

KID TESTED BY
LORALEI HOSTETLER
AGE 11

HIGHLIGHTS PRESS
HONESDALE, PENNSYLVANIA

PUNCH LINE SCAVENGER HUNT

The punch line to each of these jokes has a hidden object found somewhere in the pages of this book. Can you find them all?

HA-HA

1. WHAT DID ONE CAMPER SAY TO THE OTHER?

I can row a boat, ?

2. WHAT KIND OF CANDY IS ALWAYS LATE FOR CLASS?

A

3. WHY DO ELEPHANTS HAVE WRINKLED SKIN?

Ever tried to an elephant?

4. WHY CAN'T YOU TAKE A PICTURE OF A TIGER WITH A HAT?

Because you can't take a picture with a 🎩.

5. WHERE ARE BLACK HOLES MOST COMMONLY FOUND?

In black 🎵 s.

6. WHAT IS THE MOST DIFFICULT BEAN TO GROW?

A jelly 🫘.

7. WHAT KIND OF JEWELRY DO RABBITS WEAR?

14 gold.

HEE-HEE

2

HIDDEN PICTURES DANCE PARTY

Let DJ Pepp mix the soundtrack to your silly puzzling. Find the **6 objects** hidden in his scene, then dive into the rest of the silliest Hidden Pictures we have to offer.

Art by Jana Curll

ring

mitten

toothbrush

spoon

teacup

crescent moon

3

SPOT THE IMPOSTOR

Can you find the cow hiding among the penguins?
Can you also find the 12 hidden fish?

Why can't penguins fly?

Because they don't have a pilot's license.

Art by Travis Foster

Art by Kelly Kennedy

pennant

saw

crown

artist's brush

wristwatch

skateboard

ruler

suitcase

boot

glove

flashlight

candle

bell

toothbrush

yo-yo

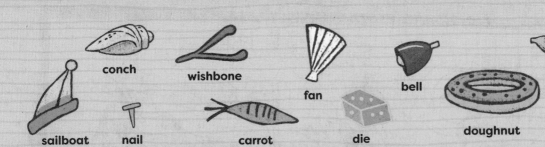

conch

wishbone

fan

bell

banana

sailboat

nail

carrot

die

doughnut

horseshoe

ladder

6

Art by Paula Bossio

7

teacup

ladder

paper airplane

domino

frying pan

envelope

ring

toothbrush

leaf

heart

candle

ice-cream cone

candy corn

8

Art by Pat Lewis

TONGUE TWISTERS

MAGNIFICENT MUSICIANSHIP.

sailboat

magnet

carrot

fishhook

mallet

flashlight

crown

drinking straw

glove

comb

ZATZ AND ZURKLE
adventures on Earth

Here's what Zatz and Zurkle called the objects they found. Can you find them, too?

upzee

flingala

sritchit

floosh

cubeedoo

glork

snoofle

krustoa

cribble

koobah

kupple

tiggly

pipo

splooshed immy

fork

tack

magnifying
glass

olive

wedge of
watermelon

ruler

slice
of pizza

worm

lighthouse

teacup

pencil

paper clip

crescent
moon

crown

toothbrush

Art by Genie Espinosa

GO SLUGGERS!

Which baseball player holds the lemonade? The pitcher.

Art by Brian Michael Weaver

canoe

paper airplane

crescent moon

cinnamon roll

spatula

cotton swab

ladder

lollipop

pencil

ruler

paper clip

skateboard

toothbrush

nail

BEARY FUNNY

To solve the first joke, start with the letter I. Then write every other letter in order on the blanks until you reach the center of the spiral, crossing out each letter once it has been used. To solve the second joke, go back to the start and write the remaining letters in order on the blanks.

START

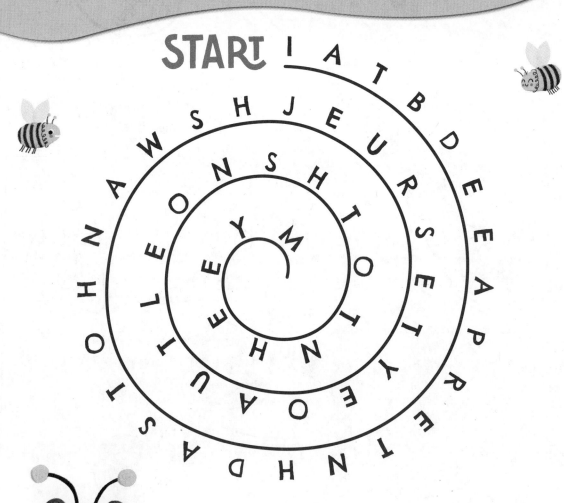

I A T B D E E A P R E T N H D A S T O H N A W S H J E U R S E I Y E O A T I E O N S H I O T N H E Y M

WHERE DO YOU FIND BLACK BEARS?

__ __   __ __ __ __ __ __

__ __ __ __   __ __ __ __ __ __

__ __ __ __   __ __ __ __ __ .

WHAT IS STRONG ON THE OUTSIDE
AND SWEET ON THE INSIDE?

__ __ __ __ __ __ __ __ __ __ __

__ __ __ __ __ __ __ __ __ __ __ __

Art by Anna Süßbauer

Art by Paula Bossio

kite · fish · comb · heart · banana · teacup · fork · tennis racket · ice-cream cone · bell · spoon · worm · pencil · slice of pizza · candle

Two goats found a roll of film and began to eat it.

"How do you like it?" asked one.

"Not bad," replied the other. "But I liked the book better."

Knock, knock.
Who's there?
Goat.
Goat who?
Goat to the door and find out!

ice-cream bar

open book

pitcher

flashlight

button

feather

envelope

Art by Brian White

flowerpot

ring

candy cane

banana

key

mitten

ice-cream cone

TONGUE TWISTERS

GREAT GRAY GOATS.

GREEDY GOATS PLUCK GRAPES.

baseball glove

paint can

slice of pizza

banana

saucepan

magnifying glass

crown

envelope

eyeglasses

paintbrush

megaphone

toothbrush

shoe

artist's brush

saw

plunger

mug

paper airplane

ring

saltshaker

ice-cream cone

Art by Travis Foster

18

SPOT THE IMPOSTOR

Can you find the squirrel hiding among the bunnies?
Can you also find 12 hidden acorns?

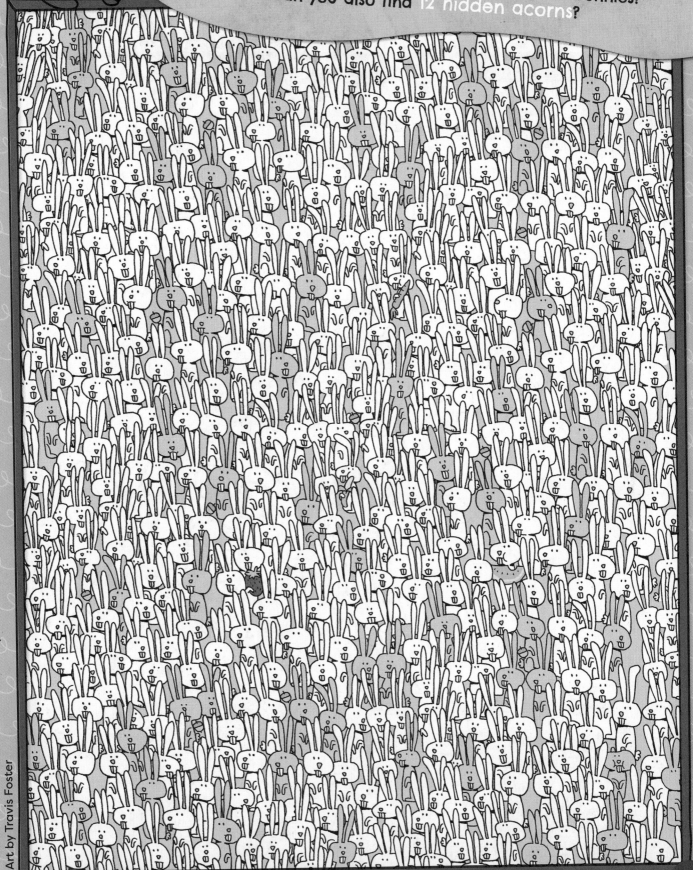

Art by Travis Foster

Pretend you're in outer space and an alien is chasing you. What should you do? Stop pretending!

PSST. IF YOU GET STUCK, HERE'S A LIST OF ALL THE OBJECTS HIDDEN IN THE SCENE.

peanut, dog bone, plunger, slice of pie, canoe, boomerang, cactus, yo-yo, lollipop, spinning top, cotton candy, ice-cream cone, potato, kazoo, wedge of cheese, hat, bowling ball

Art by Brian Micheal Weaver

A SiLLY FiLL-iN STORY

Can you find at least 12 hidden objects in the scene? As you find each object, write its name in a blank space below. Share your silly story with a friend!

My friends call me _____ the Jokester. The name is a perfect

fit for me—just like a zero-gravity _____ on a martian's

_____ ! I love to play practical jokes. Today was one of my best.

With just a pair of boots, I got the whole _____ Squad to think

that an Earthling had walked across our sandy _____ .

Ha! Could you imagine an Earthling doing that? I laughed so hard my

_____ nearly flew out of my _____ , if you can believe it!

It was better than the time I put space slime on Erkel's _____ .

Sometimes they get mad when I pull a prank. But I tell them that a

good _____ is the galaxy's best medicine. They say they weren't

sick. They might even say, " _____ !" But once they're calm again,

we all laugh and I make them a tasty _____ . I just don't tell

them a pickled _____ is the secret ingredient!

baseball bat

slice of pizza

baseball

cloud

log

kite

sailboat

pencil

cookie

lightning bolt

bacon

mitten

flashlight

window

open book

crown

bow tie

winter hat

sock

ice-cream cone

wave

mushroom

mug

leaf

party hat

paintbrush

vase

Why are camels sand-colored? For camel-flage.

We get it, Steve, you want to travel more.

Art by Joey Ellis

CHECK & DOUBLE CHECK

Find 20 differences between the two images.
BONUS: Can you find all 9 hiding friends?

Art by Esther Hernando

Don't forget to make a wish!

How do you find out a giraffe's age?
You go to its birthday party

baseball bat

piece of popcorn

teacup

eyeglasses

ring

shoe

traffic light

flag

Art by Gary LaCoste

megaphone

hat

toothbrush

fish

bowl

WORDS AND OBJECTS

The 8 objects hidden on this page match the 8 words hidden on the next page. Can you find them all?

Art by Brian White

Art by Brian White

BANANA, PEN, ARTIST'S BRUSH, KITE, LADLE, RULER, COMB, KEY

golf club

sock

strawberry

snail

kite

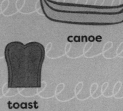
canoe

toast

lemon

CORN YOU MAKE a MATCH?

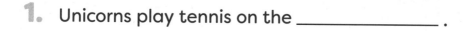

Unicorns love puns as much as the next magical creature.
To learn some of their favorite jokes, match each
riddle with its corny punch line.

1. Unicorns play tennis on the _____ .

2. Unicorns ride to the park on a _____ .

3. Unicorns love silly jokes because

   they're _____ .

4. Unicorns eat their ice cream

   in a _____ .

5. The unicorn joined the school band so

   he could wear the _____ .

6. Unicorn dads are called _____ .

7. A tiny unicorn is called a _____ .

8. Unicorns ride the merry-go-round

   at the _____ .

9. A fancy unicorn is called a _____ .

a. unicorny

b. glamicorn

c. unicourt

d. pop-corns

e. unicycle

f. unicorn-ival

g. unicone

h. uniform

i. puny-corn

SPOT THE IMPOSTOR

Can you find the octopus hiding among the fish?
Can you also find the 12 hidden shells?

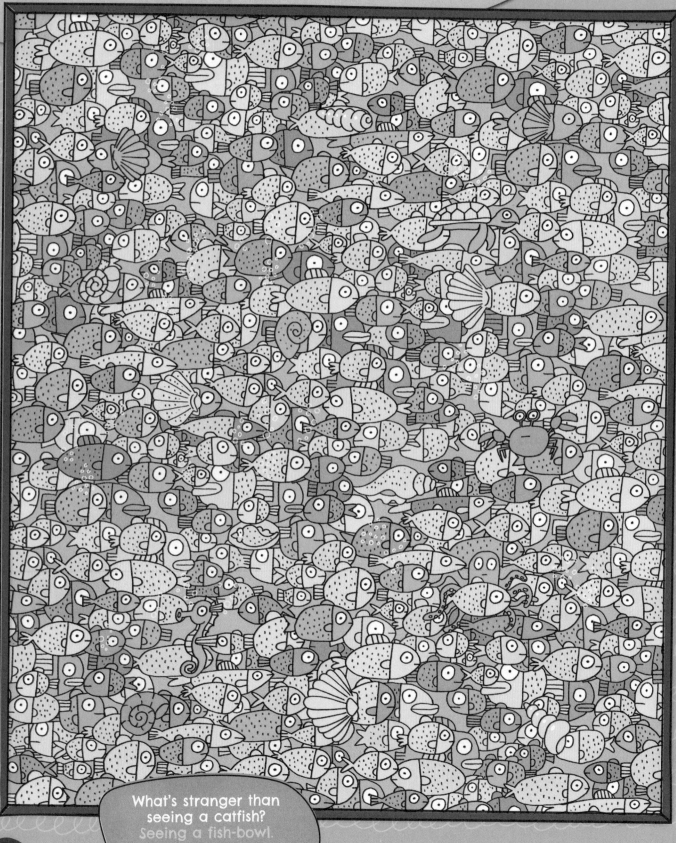

What's stranger than
seeing a catfish?
Seeing a fish-bowl.

Art by Travis Foster

light bulb ring eyeglasses artist's brush kite

crown cup heart

fork football ice-cream cone envelope slice of toast sock mushroom slice of pizza pencil

TONGUE TWISTERS
BARRY BLEW BIG, BEAUTIFUL BUBBLES.

What kind of fish likes bubble gum? A blowfish.

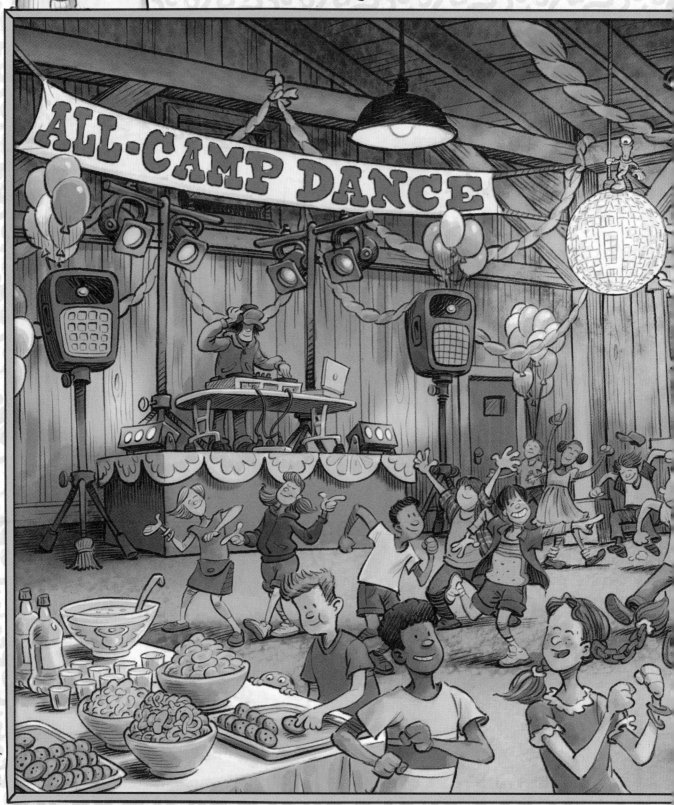

Art by Chuck Dillon

34

ZATZ AND ZURKLE
adventures on Earth

Here's what Zatz and Zurkle called the objects they found. Can you find them, too?

holdeething

stringstrong

brunchamunch

loopaloo

nodark

bitebit

joozy

butterpad

immy

headtickle

glork

sweepie

lotsarooms

If two old friends run into each other, what do they say? "Ouch!"

shoe

sock

ring

cupcake

BRACELET MAKING

frying pan

toothbrush

magnet

arrow

boot

worm

artist's brush

magnifying glass

crown

36

BEST FRIENDS DAY

crescent moon

comb

drumstick

letter E

drinking straw

cane

slice of pizza

crayon

mug

golf club

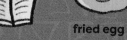
open book

fried egg

butterfly

slice of pie

ruler

wedge of orange

sailboat

banana
sock
paintbrush
pencil
spoon
toothbrush
heart
umbrella
sunglasses
wristwatch
ring
ice-cream cone
baseball
hat
slice of pizza
candy
sailboat
book
magnifying glass

Art by Luke Flowers

How long was the hamster's workout? Wheel-y long.

RULES

HOT TOWELS

Art by Kelly Kennedy

pepper

football

hammer

flag

iron

toothbrush

plunger

boot

candle

spoon

pillow

slice of pizza

artist's brush

sailboat

horseshoe

ring

eyeglasses

key

mushroom

yo-yo

PiGGY PROBLEMS

To find the answer to the riddle below, first cross out all the pairs of matching letters. Then write the remaining letters in order in the spaces beneath the riddle.

KK	SS	AA	TH	TT	RR	BB	EP
CC	IG	NN	LL	MM	ZZ	HA	II
PP	YY	GG	VV	DT	EE	LL	CC
OS	TT	XX	WW	QQ	TA	KK	HH
OO	EE	RT	JJ	YY	AA	NN	US
RR	PP	CC	IN	TT	SS	QQ	KK
GA	WW	UU	ZZ	BB	MM	PE	GG
II	LL	FF	NC	QQ	HH	DD	IL

WHAT HAPPENED WHEN THE PIG PEN BROKE?

___ ___ ___ ___ ___ ___ ___

___ ___ ___ ___ ___ ___ ___

___ ___ ___ ___ .

A SiLLY FiLL-iN STORY

Can you find at least 11 hidden objects in the scene? As you find each object, write its name in a blank space below. Share your silly story with a friend!

We are visiting Paris for the first time today. We rode a _____

to the Louvre, the biggest _____ in the world. My favorite

_____ was the Mona _____. At a nearby patisserie,

Dad bought everyone a _____—and at the last minute he

bought himself a big _____, too. That afternoon, we went to

see the Eiffel Tower. It's taller than a _____! Mom and Dad

pulled out their _____ to take a picture. My sister and I couldn't

believe our _____. Mom pretended to hold the Eiffel Tower

while Dad took her _____. They are so embarassing.

Just your typical _____ vacation, I guess!

Andy:
Good news! I've saved up enough money for us to go to Paris this summer.

Rachel:
Wonderful! When are we going to leave?

Andy:
As soon as I've saved enough for us to come back.

HiDDEN PICTURES TAKE TWO

Each of these scenes contains 12 hidden objects, which are listed on the next page. Find each object in ONE of the scenes, then cross it off the list.

Art by Brian Michael Weaver

EACH OBJECT IS HIDDEN ONLY ONCE. CAN YOU FIND THEM ALL?

acorn	carrot	heart	piece of popcorn
adhesive bandage	crescent moon	hockey stick	ruler
artist's brush	envelope	ice-cream bar	spoon
banana	eyeglasses	lollipop	tack
baseball cap	fishing net	needle	top hat
broccoli	harmonica	olive	wishbone

45

SPOT THE IMPOSTOR

Can you find the turtle hiding among the frogs?
Can you also find the 12 hidden flies?

Why are frogs always happy? Because they eat whatever bugs them.

Art by Travis Foster

47

nail
rake
plane
ladle
party hat
plate
snail
cane
snake
cake

I'm nuts about you guys!

pencil

slice of pizza

banana

strawberry

muffin

gingerbread man

key

jar

ice-cream bar

ice-cream cone

boot

crown

candle

fish

pyramid

present

pencil

glove

key

heart

baseball

What's a bird's favorite snack?
Potato cheeps.

Art by Hector Borlasca

TONGUE TWISTERS
THE CAT ATTACKED A STACK OF SNACKS.

ghost

magnifying glass

pencil

flashlight

ladder

crown

ice-cream cone

sailboat

tennis ball

domino

ruler

wristwatch

fish

ring

butterfly

comb

Art by Hazel Quintanilla

What kind of pizza makes people sneeze?
Pepper-only pizza.

A SiLLY FiLL-iN STORY

Can you find at least 12 hidden objects in the scene? As you find each object, write its name in a blank space below. Share your silly story with a friend!

Firestone Pizza is the best _____ joint in town. We only

use the freshest ingredients. We pick the _____ off the vine

for our _____ and milk our own _____ to make our

_____ . And if you love the brick _____ pizza taste,

no one does it better than us! As long as you don't mind a little

spit when we breathe _____ into the oven. Our chefs love

to experiment with exciting pizza toppings, like the fan favorite

_____ and _____ . That pizza was even given the

Best _____ Award by our local news station, _____

News. A high onor! So come try something new at our restaurant

today. We promise you won't leave

with an empty _____ !

55

BAKE SALE

Just one more stinky salmon cupcake?

crescent moon

feather

ladder

umbrella

slice of watermelon

crown

slice of pizza

artist's brush

eyeglasses

domino

fishhook

candle

heart

key

comb

ring

toothbrush

paper clip

ice-cream cone

peanut

shoe

ice pop

sock

drinking straw

Art by Gina Perry

56

PIN the BANANA

Art by Josh Cleland

BONUS
HOW MANY
BANANAS CAN YOU
FIND IN THE SCENE?

AQUATIC HUMOR

To solve the first joke, start with the letter A. Then write every other letter in order on the blanks until you reach the center of the spiral, crossing out each letter once it has been used. To solve the second joke, go back to the start and write the remaining letters in order on the blanks.

START

Spiral letters (from START inward):
A T S H W E O C R A D S A E N I D Y H S E A D S I T P O F T I A S H N B W E A C S A G L O W N A T Y C R K P

WHAT IS THE BEST-DRESSED FISH IN THE OCEAN?

_ _____, ____ ____

__'_ _____ _____.

WHY DIDN'T THE MAN PLAY CARDS DURING THE OCEAN CRUISE?

___ ___ ___

_____ __ ___ ____.

58

Can you find all **8 hidden jelly beans** in this scene?

SPOT THE IMPOSTOR

Can you find the dumpling hiding among the sushi?
Can you also find the 12 hidden shrimp?

Brett: Want to try that 50% off sushi?
Ari: I don't know, it sounds fishy to me.

Art by Erica Sirotich

sock

ladle

baseball bat

cloud

toothbrush

puzzle piece

bow

paper airplane

wedge of lime

teacup

strawberry

nail

ruler

saltshaker

plate

frying pan

envelope

TONGUE TWISTERS

SO THIS IS THE SINGING SUSHI CHEF?

Art by Jana Curll

61

WORDS AND OBJECTS

The 8 objects hidden on this page match the 8 words hidden on the next page. Can you find them all?

Art by Brian White

BANANA, CANE, CROWN, FORK, GLOVE, LEAF, MUG, RULER

Art by Brian White

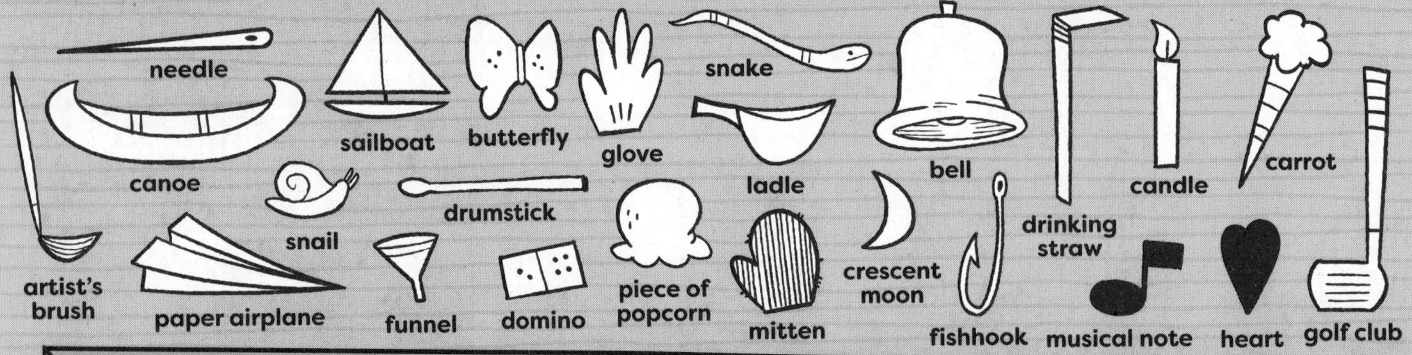

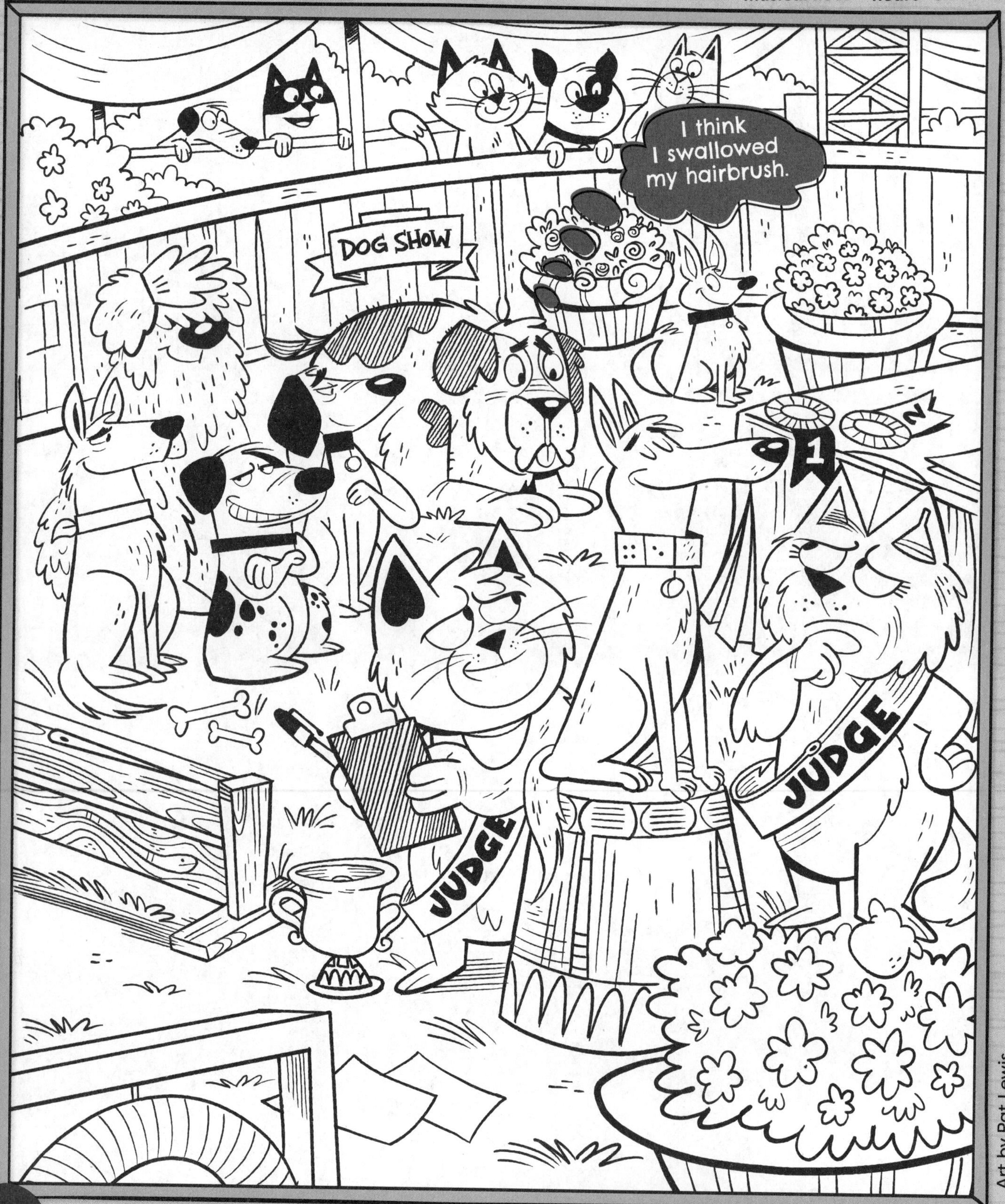

Art by Pat Lewis

Art by Gideon Kendall

That's easy—because they're delicious!

Here's what Zatz and Zurkle called the objects they found. Can you find them, too?

joozy

sweepina

fuzzer

snipsnip

glowslice

gleep

headtickle

howlongz

prettywing

hedshine

floosh

hosenose

What's worse than raining cats and dogs? Hailing taxi cabs!

Art by Kelly Kennedy

fish

slice of pizza

ring

hammer

magnet

ruler

nail

ghost

saltshaker

skateboard

canoe

glove

hockey stick

magnifying glass

worm

belt

artist's brush

wedge of lemon

pitcher

WACKY NEW DOG BREEDS

You've heard of a golden retriever, but have you heard of these silly dog breeds? To find out which dog breed is which, match up these riddles with their punch lines.

What kind of dog . . .

1. doesn't bark?

2. says *meow*?

3. likes baths?

4. loves to play football?

5. can tell time?

6. washes clothes?

7. loves science?

8. needs gloves?

9. is solid as cement?

10. do vampires have?

a. A golden receiver

b. A laundro-mutt

c. An undercover police dog

d. A lab

e. A rock-weiler

f. A bloodhound

g. A hot dog

h. A clocker spaniel

i. A sham-poodle

j. A boxer

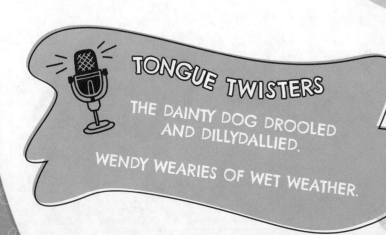

TONGUE TWISTERS

THE DAINTY DOG DROOLED AND DILLYDALLIED.

WENDY WEARIES OF WET WEATHER.

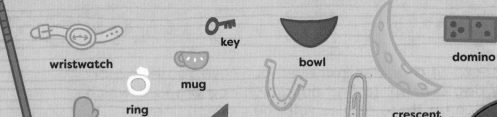

wristwatch

key

bowl

domino

ring

mug

mitten

horseshoe

crescent mooon

golf club

pencil

sailboat

envelope

paper clip

heart

Knock, knock.
Who's there?
Axolotl.
Axolotl who?
Did you axolotl people to your birthday party?

Art by Mitch Mortimer

TONGUE TWISTERS

SNAKES SLURP SLIPPERY NOODLES.

hourglass

ring

open book

light bulb

crescent moon

piece of popcorn

saw

banana

question mark

key

knitted hat

football

broccoli

baseball bat

plunger

carrot

slice of watermelon

whistle

When is a dog not a dog? When it's a pet.

A BOOK NEVER WRITTEN:
Bathing Your Cat
by Manny Scratches

belt

scissors

baseball bat

button

bowl

magnet

ice-cream cone

pencil

bread

ladder

banana

bean

spring

fork

72

slice of pizza

slice of watermelon

ruler

die

doughnut

needle

frying pan

glove

ring

spoon

fish

cane

bowling ball

SPOT THE IMPOSTOR

Can you find the dog hiding among the cats?
Can you also find the 12 hidden mice?

Art by Travis Foster

A SiLLY FiLL-iN STORY

Can you find at least 11 hidden objects in the scene? As you find each object, write its name in a blank space below. Share your silly story with a friend!

Eight Reasons Why Pigs Shouldn't Be Plumbers

1. Pigs aren't allowed to go to _____ school to learn how to use a _____ .

2. They take too many extra breaks to eat their _____ -and- _____ sandwiches.

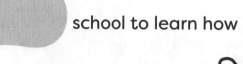

3. They can't reach the top of a kitchen _____ .

4. Their idea of paradise is a mud pit with food scraps and a smelly _____ to boot!

5. They sing, "Who's Afraid of the Big Bad _____ !" so loud it could make a _____ burst.

6. They believe a plunger should be used as a _____ .

7. Pigs think a dripping _____ is better if it leaks a lot.

8. They'll add mud and turn your _____ into a pig party!

bell

canoe

needle

mushroom

sock

spatula

envelope

golf club

carrot

baseball

sailboat

candy cane

wedge of lemon

ring

dinosaur

What do you call an almond in outer space? An astro-nut.

Art by Gary LaCoste

Art by Mike Lowery

pencil
bowling ball
toothbrush
waffle
bowl
slice of pizza
snail
crown
ruler
snake
crescent moon
candle
lollipop

WHАT'S WRONG?

What things are silly in this picture? It's up to you!

BONUS
HOW MANY BUBBLES CAN YOU FIND IN THE SCENE?

Art by Annika Brandow

In that case— let's get lost, Zatz!

ZATZ AND ZURKLE
adventures on Earth

Here's what Zatz and Zurkle called the objects they found. Can you find them, too?

outview

slowgo

clipclop

offugo

skyhighs

boingboing

holdit

headtickle

owzie

colorator

upzee

seemore

clickclack

To find the answer to the riddle below, first cross out all the pairs of matching letters. Then write the remaining letters in order in the spaces beneath the riddle.

WW NN WI OO CC LL DD

SS UU YY EE TH AA MM

HH AN BB II FF WW EX

AA MM FF PE CC RR VV

LL RI QQ OO GG SS JJ

RR DD ZZ PP MI XX HH

EE JJ II NT TT YY AA

HOW DOES A SCIENCE TEACHER
FRESHEN THEIR BREATH?

___ __ __ __ __ __ -

___ __ __ __ __ __ __ __ __ -

___ __ __ __ __ __ __ .

TONGUE TWISTERS

THE SCIENTIST'S EXPERIMENT
EXCEEDED EXPECTATIONS.

THE CLASS CLOCK CLICKED CLEARLY.

Art by James Lancett

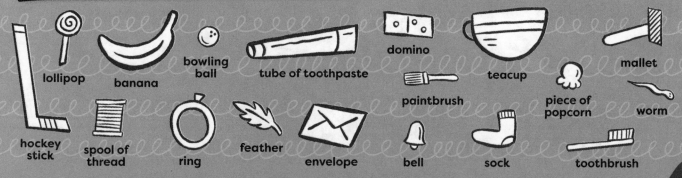

lollipop

banana

bowling ball

tube of toothpaste

domino

teacup

mallet

paintbrush

piece of popcorn

worm

hockey stick

spool of thread

ring

feather

envelope

bell

sock

toothbrush

envelope

waffle

cinnamon roll

briefcase

crown

ruler

comb

bone

ring

banana

candy corn

open book

marker

spoon

slice of pizza

drum

heart

nail

wishbone

teacup

toothbrush

candy cane

slice of watermelon

lollipop

bow tie

dinosaur

SPOT THE IMPOSTOR

Can you find the possum hiding among the bats?
Can you also find the 12 hidden spiders?

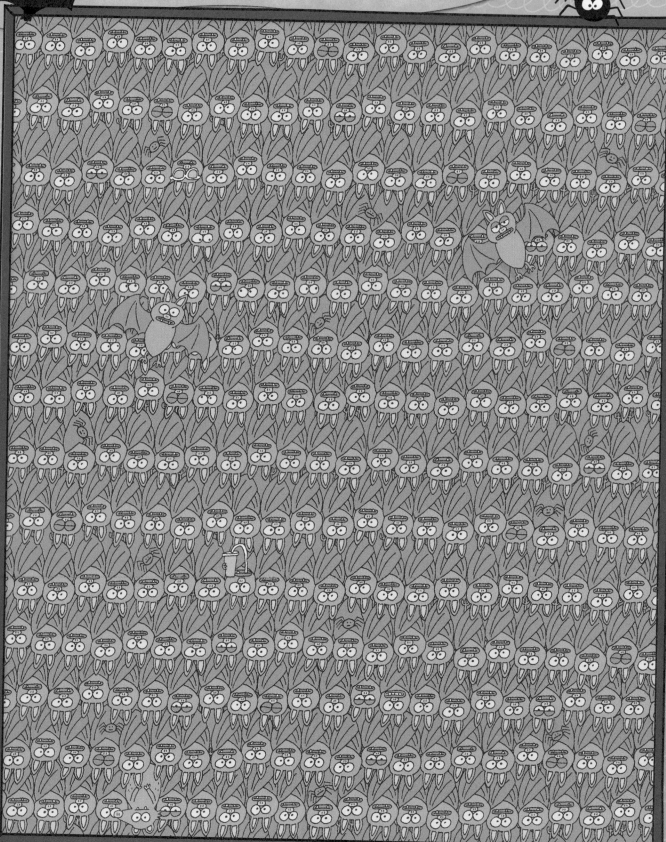

Art by Travis Foster

domino

boot

golf club

bow tie

paintbrush

flag

popcorn

fork

toothbrush

candle

button

closed umbrella

horseshoe

flying saucer

fish

pointy hat

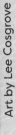

Art by Lee Cosgrove

One day, a bat left to get food and returned with a huge bump on his head.

First bat: What happened?
Second bat: You see that tree over there?
First bat: Yes.
Second bat: Well, I didn't.

candy cane

lollipop

domino

open book

banana

glove

crown

pencil

hockey stick

ladle

slice of toast

acorn

fork

candy corn

envelope

ladder

button

comb

barbell

paintbrush

needle

candle

can

Damian: My dog plays chess.
Laurie: Your dog must be really smart!
Damian: Oh, I don't know. I usually win two out of three times.

90

Art by Pat Lewis

Knock, knock.
Who's there?
Goose.
Goose who?
No, you goose who!

Art by Paula Becker

heart
baseball
mug
fried egg
comb
crown
lollipop
fork
cinnamon roll
ring
crescent moon
sock
tack
lemon
horseshoe
belt
caterpillar

TONGUE TWISTERS

IF GOOSE GOES TO GEESE, DO TWO MOOSE MAKE MEESE?

Art by Rich Powell

vase

pretzel

ax

drinking
straw

canoe

envelope

hockey stick

A BOOK NEVER WRITTEN:
Delicious Breakfast Foods
by Chris P. Bacon

bottle

sock

feather

chef's hat

hanger

button

toothbrush

slice of pizza

baseball bat

comb

heart

hat

ruler

slice of cheese

crescent moon

glove

fishhook

93

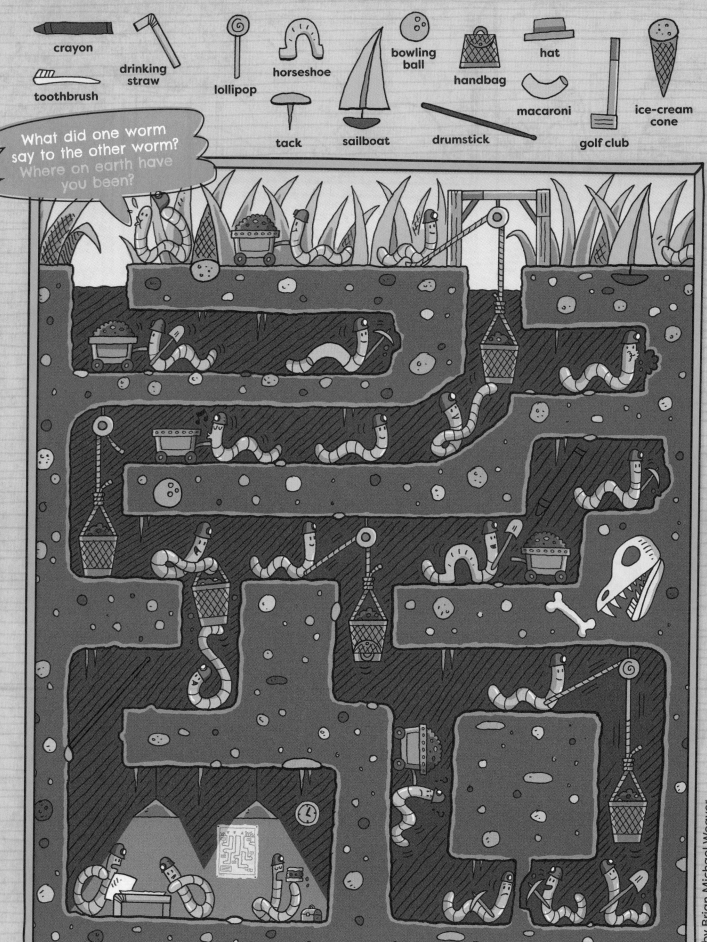

94

banana, toothbrush, safety pin, envelope, frying pan, magnifying glass, button, peanut, lightning bolt, turkey drumstick, whale

PSST. IF YOU GET STUCK, HERE'S A LIST OF ALL THE OBJECTS HIDDEN IN THE SCENE.

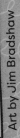

A SiLLY FiLL-iN STORY

Can you find 11 hidden objects in the scene?
As you find each object, write its name in a blank
space below. Share your silly story with a friend!

Sisters Violetta and Rosetta woke up in their _____ feeling sad.

Their cousins were flying in a _____ to an amusement _____

for a week, and the sisters wished they could go. Farmer Eugene saw

how upset they were and had a great _____. "Come along for a

_____ today, girls," he said. The sisters hopped onto his tractor,

and the three rode across the _____. Each _____ in the

road, the girls flew up in the _____ and then landed with a thud.

They laughed and yelled, "Again!" Farmer Eugene drove faster over the

_____, and the cows and _____ watched as the sisters flew

higher and higher. By the end of the day, Violetta and Rosetta didn't feel

quite so sad they hadn't gone with their cousins.

Who needs an amusement _____

when you live on a farm?

Art by Gary LaCoste

How does a sloth make dinner? With a slow cooker.

TONGUE TWISTERS
SIX SLOW SNAILS SLID SILENTLY.

SLIPPERY WHEN SLIMY

balloon

baseball

sailboat

toothbrush

pencil

banana

mitten

ice-cream cone

needle

tack

envelope

fishhook

heart

carrot

bell

hockey stick

paper airplane   traffic cone   ice-cream cone   slice of pie   sailboat

sandwich   traffic sign   slice of pizza

YOU'RE THE TOPS!

You've heard of *Triceratops*, but have you heard of these sillysaurs? To find out which dinosaur is which, match up these riddles with their punch lines.

Which dinosaur . . .

1. cleans the floor?

2. loves to trampoline?

3. waits at traffic lights?

4. slices and dices food?

5. is the best police officer?

6. can't hold on to things?

7. loves to buy things?

8. gives great compliments?

9. is a terrific grandfather?

10. makes a big splash in a pool?

a. Tricera-chops

b. Tricera-cops

c. Tricera-drops

d. Tricera-flops

e. Tricera-hops

f. Tricera-mops

g. Tricera-pops

h. Tricera-props

i. Tricera-shops

j. Tricera-stops

TONGUE TWISTERS

SHIRLEY, I'M CERTAIN THAT STEGOSAURUS SAW US.

T. REX TRIPPED TWICE.

Art by Josh Cleland

What is the best time to go to the dentist? Tooth-hurty.

Art by Jim Bertram

heart · sock · bird · comb · baseball cap · pencil · paw print · musical note · banana · saltshaker · carrot · pointy hat · golf club

SPOT THE IMPOSTOR

Can you find the octopus hiding among the sea stars?
Can you also find the 12 hidden seashells?

Art by Travis Foster

WHAT'S WRONG?

What things are silly in this picture? It's up to you!

Art by David Arumi

BONUS
HOW MANY BUGS CAN YOU FIND IN THE SCENE?

padlock

slice of pizza

fork

kite

bowl

toothbrush

dog bone

spoon

golf club

ruler

saucepan

suitcase

can

ring

magnet

broom

teapot

WORDS AND OBJECTS

The 8 objects hidden on this page match the 8 words hidden on the next page. Can you find them all?

Art by Howard McWilliam

ARROW, LOLLIPOP, COAT HANGER, PENCIL, RULER, SLICE OF PIZZA, BALLOON, LEMON

Art by Howard McWilliam

SPLOOSH

DIRTY DISHES ←

MILK
MILK
MILK
MILK
MILK

What do you call the rear of the lunchroom?
A bacteria.

pencil

tack

heart

sock

mushroom

needle

bell

envelope

boomerang

ball of yarn

golf club

ladle

paper clip

crown

slice of lemon

ice-cream cone

canoe

bowl

banana

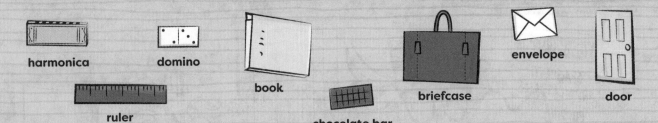

harmonica

domino

book

briefcase

envelope

ruler

chocolate bar

door

Art by Tamara Petrosino

Art by Hector Borlasca

football
heart
domino
teacup
slice of pizza
wedge of lime
artist's brush
marker
ice-cream cone

ring
lollipop
crown
slice of toast
open book
slice of watermelon
paint can
fish

Art by Ron Lieser

PSST. IF YOU GET STUCK, HERE'S A LIST OF ALL THE OBJECTS HIDDEN IN THE SCENE.

sock, candle, caterpillar, flag, wishbone, fishhook, snake, mallet, cane, canoe, lollipop, golf club

A SiLLY FiLL-iN STORY

Can you find at least 11 hidden objects in the scene? As you find each object, write its name in a blank space below. Share your silly story with a friend!

It is with great pleasure that I accept the title, "Pig of the Year." My

grandfather, Swinegustus _____ Hog, once held this honor. I am

proud to follow him. Friends, I like to eat the last piece of _____

in the trough, I like to roll in _____-scented mud, and I love

a good _____ in the morning. But there is nothing I like more

than winning this honor. So I vow to put more _____ in each of

our bellies, to cover the _____ with more mud (You can never

have too much mud, can you?), and to build the best _____

our farm has ever seen. I will make this year the best that it can be.

Remember my slogan, "An extra _____ in our troughs! Another

_____ in our stalls!" I promise this to every pig in this farm,

or my name is not _____ X. Hambone. Thanks

to each and every _____ in the audience!

needle

flag   fishhook   drinking straw   pencil

sailboat   football

artist's brush   piece of popcorn   lightning bolt   heart   tack   crescent moon   basketball   carrot   bell   candle

Art by Gary LaCoste

NOW YOU SEE ME

To solve the first joke, start with the letter D. Then write every other letter in order on the blanks until you reach the center of the spiral, crossing out each letter once it has been used. To solve the second joke, go back to the start and write the remaining letters in order on the blanks.

START D B O E N C T A W L A L I B N C S M U O S R E A S N L O A S P R T E E I Y A G S N H K

WHAT DID THE MOM CHAMELEON SAY TO HER NERVOUS KID ON THE FIRST DAY OF SCHOOL?

_ _ _ ' _   _ _ _ _ _ _ ,   _ _ _ ' _ _

_ _ _ _ _   _ _ _ _ _   _ _ !

WHY SHOULDN'T YOU PLAY HIDE-AND-SEEK WITH A MOUNTAIN?

_ _ _ _ _ _ _   _ _ _ _ _

_ _ _ _ _ _ _ .

115

SPOT THE IMPOSTOR

Can you find the pepper hiding among the avocados?
Can you also find the 12 hidden tortilla chips?

Art by Erica Sirotich

Each of these scenes contains 12 hidden objects, which are listed on the next page. Find each object in ONE of the scenes, then cross it off the list.

Art by Brian White

What do elephants wear on their legs? Ele-pants.

Art by Brian White

EACH OBJECT IS HIDDEN ONLY ONCE. CAN YOU FIND THEM ALL?

banana	fishhook	ice-cream cone	ruler
candle	fried egg	paper clip	slice of lime
cane	glove	paper airplane	slice of pie
carrot	golf club	pear	strawberry
crown	heart	pencil	tent
envelope	horseshoe	ring	toothbrush

envelope

magnifying glass

ball of yarn

crayon

golf club

stapler

wedge of orange

worm

crown

flag   magnet   toothbrush   paper clip   T-square   boomerang   mushroom   leaf   hot dog

cane

toothbrush

cookie

ladder

banana

iron

grapes

baseball bat

key

spoon

book

toothbrush

envelope

duck

slice of toast

crayon

flag

teapot

mitten

ruler

saltshaker

pencil

comb

musical note

HOT ROD

To find the answer to the riddle below, first cross out all the pairs of matching letters. Then write the remaining letters in order in the spaces beneath the riddle.

WW II AS AA LL PP EE
CC XX GG ZZ YY TA BB
OO TI FF KK QQ HH NN
SS KK TT DD ON UU YY
DR AA HH BB II VV OO
MM UU PP AG WW GG RR
LL JJ EE SS NN ON DD

WHAT DO YOU CALL A CAR THAT BREATHES FIRE?

___ _ _ _ _ _ _ _

_ _ _ _ _ _ _ _ _ .

TONGUE TWISTERS

THE DRAGON DRAGS THE RUSTY RED WAGON.

NO GNOMES KNOW THE WAY HOME.

Art by Mar Ferrero

SPARKY

Why did the dragon cheer? He was fired up

ice-cream cone

ghost

wedge of lemon

fish

crown

teacup

crayon

candy cane

magnet

candy corn

umbrella

drinking straw

bowling ball

football

balloon

thimble

candle

PSST. IF YOU GET STUCK, HERE'S A LIST OF ALL THE OBJECTS HIDDEN IN THE SCENE.

sailboat, sock, slice of pizza, wedge of lemon, golf club, needle, cane, bowl, dinosaur, hockey stick, fishhook, traffic light, fish, bell, ladle, flag, flashlight, ring

A SiLLY FiLL-iN STORY

Can you find at least 16 hidden objects in the scene? As you find each object, write its name in a blank space below. Share your silly story with a friend!

Dear _____ :

Please excuse my _____ from school tomorrow. As you may know,

our family was recently contacted by the head _____ at NASA

and asked to participate in a space/time experiment. So we and our pet

_____ will be traveling into the future tomorrow. We will probably

end up on the planet _____ -20 in the Alpha- _____ solar

system in the _____ galaxy. By the way, all the teachers there

happen to be _____ s with five _____ s and 20 _____ s!

You would so fit in! It will certainly be a _____ experience, and I hope

you agree. The plan is for my _____ to bring some _____ s

back from the trip for _____ -and-tell at school. If all goes

well, my _____ should be back in school by _____ !

Thank you.

hockey stick

flowerpot

candle

yo-yo

muffin

sailboat

bottle

comb

domino

paper clip

musical note

pencil

Taco 'bout a good game!

mitten

fan

crescent moon

mug

boomerang

button

drumstick

Art by James Loram

toothbrush   cloud   belt   key   ruler

ring

skateboard

eyeglasses

heart

candle

crayon

can

ladle

shoe

bowl

wishbone

mitten

boomerang

cupcake

musical note

toothbrush

ladder

Art by Pat Lewis

PUNCH LINE SCAVENGER HUNT

Page 2

1. CANOE, PAGE 64;
2. CHOCOLATE BAR, PAGE 110;
3. IRON, PAGE 122;
4. HAT, PAGE 27;
5. SOCK, PAGE 108;
6. BEAN, PAGE 109;
7. CARROT, PAGE 71

Page 3

Page 4

Page 5

Page 6

Page 7

What is a clock's favorite birthday gift?
The present.

Pages 8–9

ANSWERS

Pages 10–11

Page 12

Page 13

BEARY FUNNY

Page 14

Where do you find black bears?
It depends on where you lost them.

What is strong on the outside and
sweet on the inside?
A bear that has just eaten honey.

Page 15

Pages 16–17

Page 18

Page 19

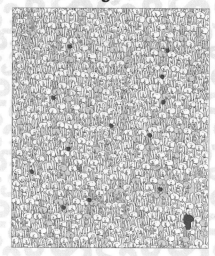

Pages 20–21

Page 22

Page 23

Page 24

Page 25

Pages 26–27

ANSWERS

Page 28

Page 29

Page 30

CORN YOU MAKE A MATCH?

Page 31

1. c, 2. e, 3. a, 4. g, 5. h,
6. d, 7. i, 8. f, 9. b

Page 32

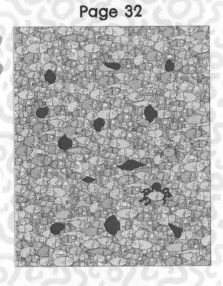

Page 33

Pages 34–35

Pages 36–37

Page 38

Page 39

Page 40

PIGGY PROBLEMS

Page 41

What happened when the pig pen broke?

The pig had to start using a pencil.

Pages 42–43

Page 44

Page 45

ANSWERS

Page 46

Page 47

Page 48

Page 49

Pages 50-51

Page 52

Page 53

Pages 54-55

Page 56

AQUATIC HUMOR

Page 58

What is the best-dressed
fish in the ocean?
A swordfish, because
it's always sharp.

Why didn't the man play cards
during the ocean cruise?
The captain was standing
on the deck.

Page 59

Page 60

Page 61

Page 62

Page 63

Page 64

Page 65

ANSWERS

Pages 66–67

Page 68

WACKY NEW DOG BREEDS

Page 69

1. g, 2. c, 3. i, 4. a, 5. h, 6. b,
7. d, 8. j, 9. e, 10. f

Page 70

Page 71

Pages 72–73

Page 74

Page 75

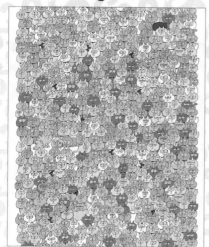

Pages 76–77

Page 78

Page 79

Page 80

SCIENCE CLASS LAUGHS

Page 84

How does a science teacher freshen their breath? With an experi-mint.

Pages 82–83

Page 85

ANSWERS

Pages 86–87

Page 88

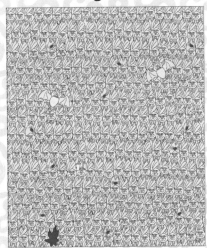

Page 89

Page 90

Page 91

Pages 92–93

Page 94

Page 95

Pages 96–97

Page 98

Page 99

Page 100

YOU'RE THE TOPS!

Page 101

1. f, 2. e, 3. j, 4. a, 5. b,
6. c, 7. i, 8. h, 9. g, 10. d

Page 102

Page 103
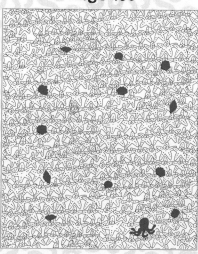

Page 105

ANSWERS

Page 106

Page 107

Pages 108–109

Page 110

Page 111

Pages 112–113

Page 114

NOW YOU SEE ME

Page 115
What did the mom chameleon say to her nervous kid on the first day of school?
Don't worry, you'll blend right in!
Why shouldn't you play hide-and-seek with a mountain?
Because mountains always peak

Page 116

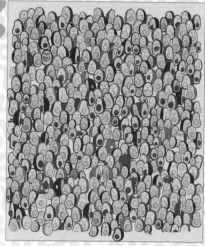

Page 117

Page 118

Page 119

Pages 120-121

Page 122

ANSWERS

HOT ROD

Page 124
What do you call a car
that breathes fire?
A station dragon.

Page 123

Page 125

Pages 126–127

Pages 128–129

Page 130

For information about permission to reprint selections from
this book, please contact permissions@highlights.com.

COVER ART BY
JANA CURLL

Doodle art by Sebastian Abboud, except on page 55:
lineartestpilot, MartinaVaculikova; pages 62–63: cako74,
ourlifelooklikeballoon; page 88: ArtnLera; page 106:
Dedy Setyawan; page 107: ElenaLux; page 113:
FrankRamspott; page 118: Mikaila Ulmer, Getty Images

Published by Highlights Press
815 Church Street,
Honesdale, Pennsylvania 18431
Printed in Mattoon, IL, USA
Mfg. 10/2023
ISBN: 978-1-63962-152-1

First edition
Visit our website at Highlights.com.
10 9 8 7 6 5 4 3 2 1